And Then I Fell Asleep

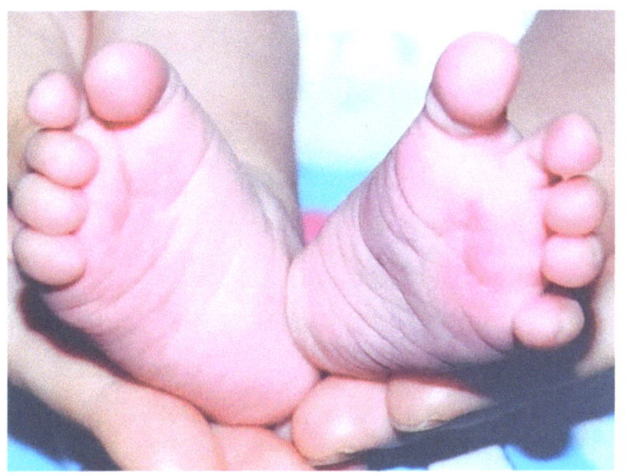

TAMMY BYRNE

ISBN 979-8-89026-787-0

Praises for Jaisal

And Then I Fell Asleep

“I couldn’t stop crying”

“This book is truly about mummy’s love for her little boy”

“I don’t know how she finds the strength, but she is so strong to write these words for her little boy”

“A book to cherish for life in honour of little Jaisal”

“Sleep well little boy. Mummy will forever love you”

“We all miss you very much, our special boy”

And Then I Fell Asleep

Thank You

The little boy and his mummy would like to dedicate this book to-

Grandpa and Api for their consistent support, blessings, love and prayers

To the little boy's aunties for showering so much love

To Aunty Doreen, Aunty Hoinu, the doctors and nurses at the hospitals in New Delhi and Imphal, India

To all their extended family for their understanding and support

Above all, to God for the abundant blessings, strength and courage.

"Ours for a little while,

In heaven forever"

There once was a little boy who lived in his little world,
Surrounded by love and love alone.
He had all his toys and all his beautiful books,
But the most favourite of all was his mummy's phone.

His magenta and grey elephant
Was his favourite toy.
It calmed him down so quickly.
His mummy would say,
“What a good boy!”

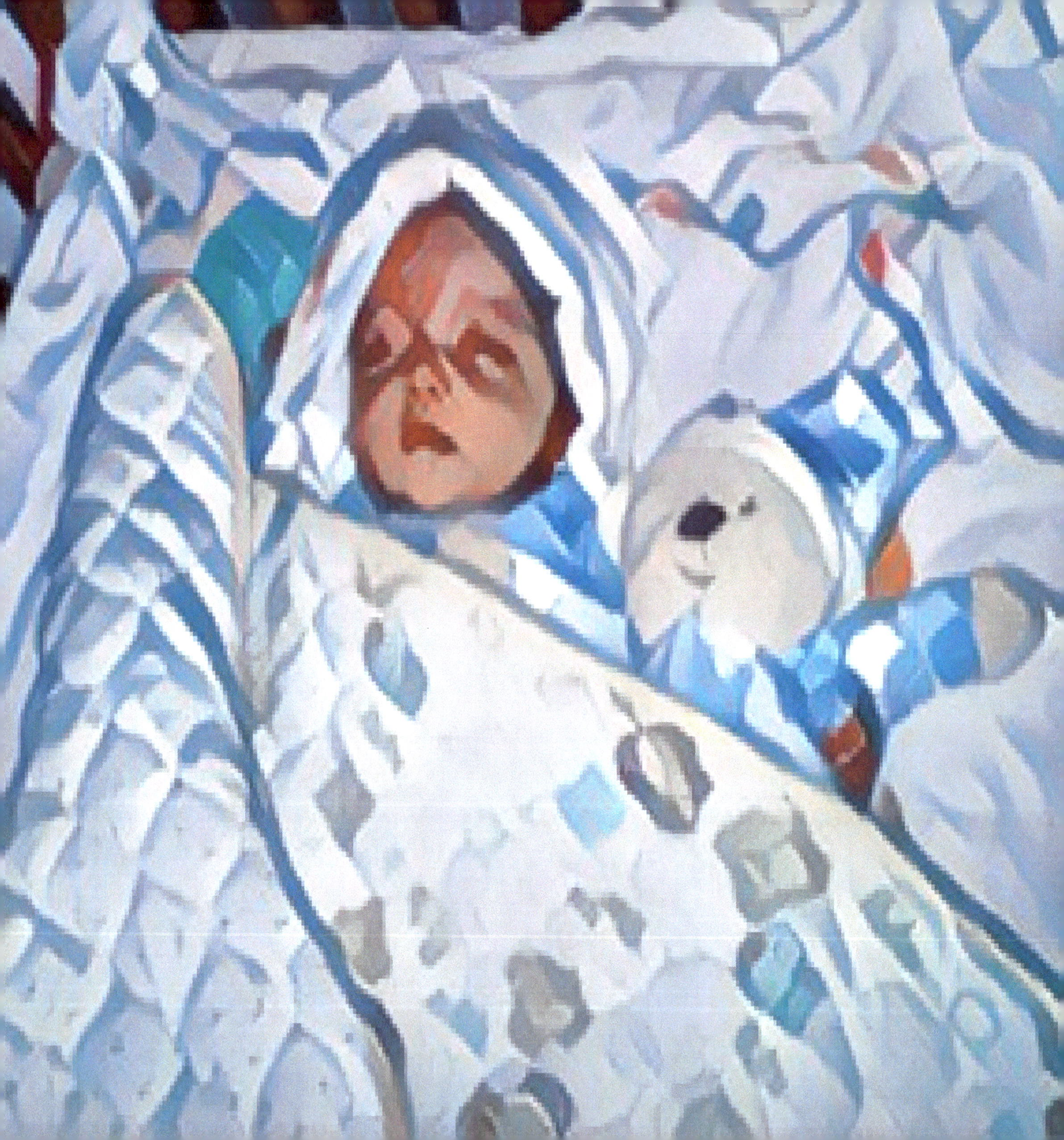

The blue teddy was his other beloved toy.
He cuddled them everyday,
And they both brought him great joy!

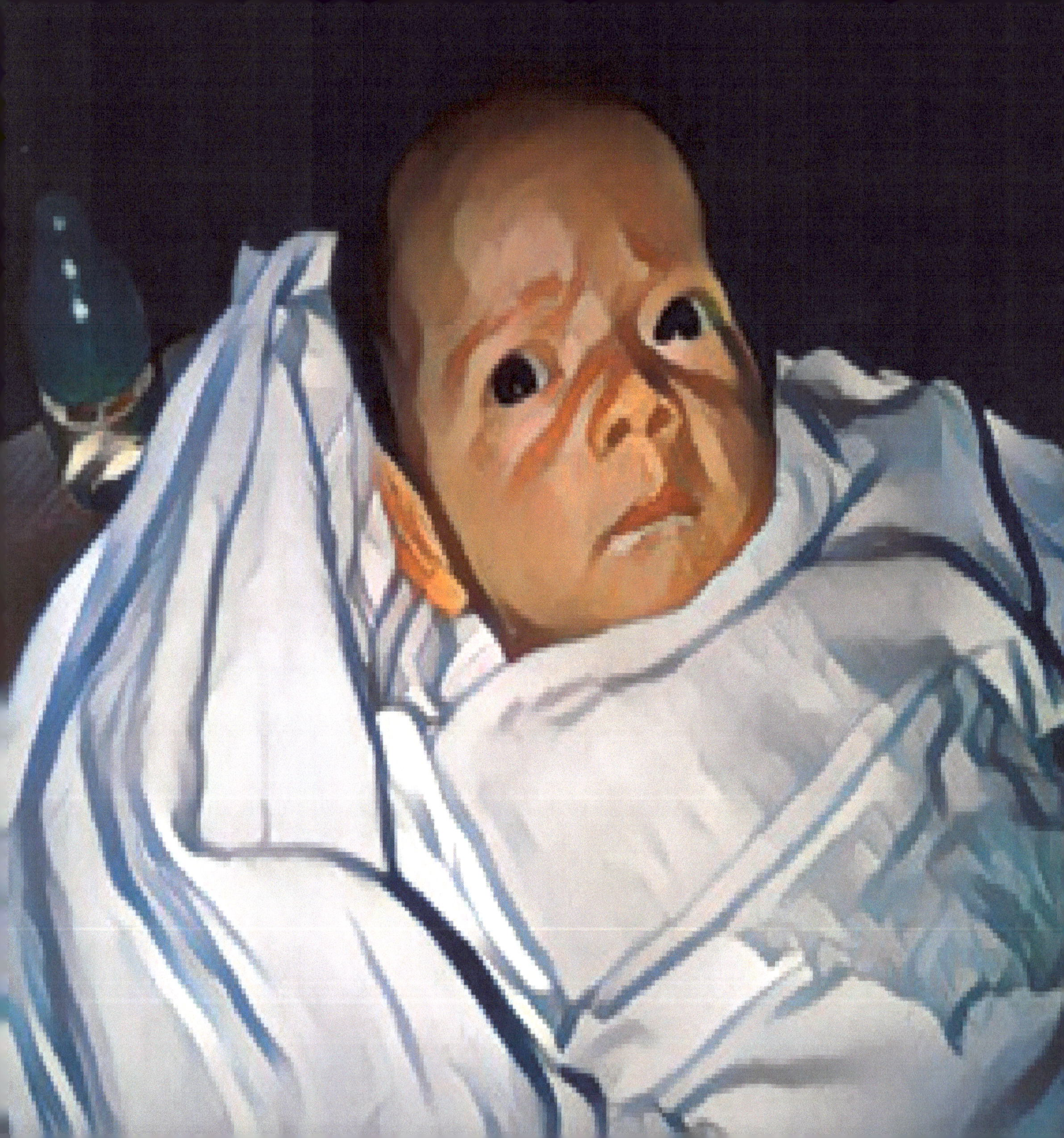

On a cold, windy day
The little boy fell poorly.
So off he went to the doctors
Wrapped warm, with his mummy.

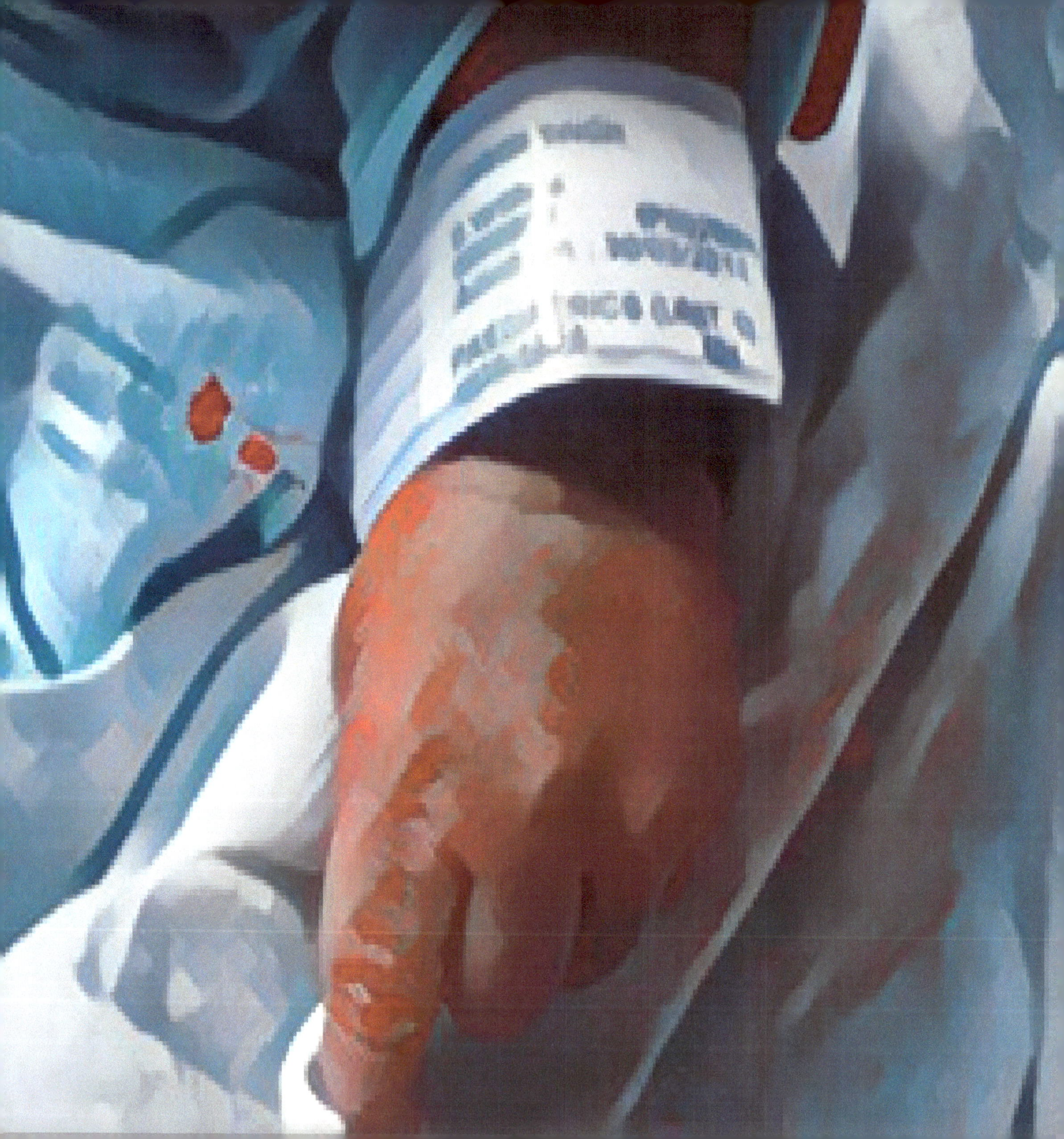

After pricking and prodding
Scanning and testing,
The doctors told mummy,
“It might be his tummy.”

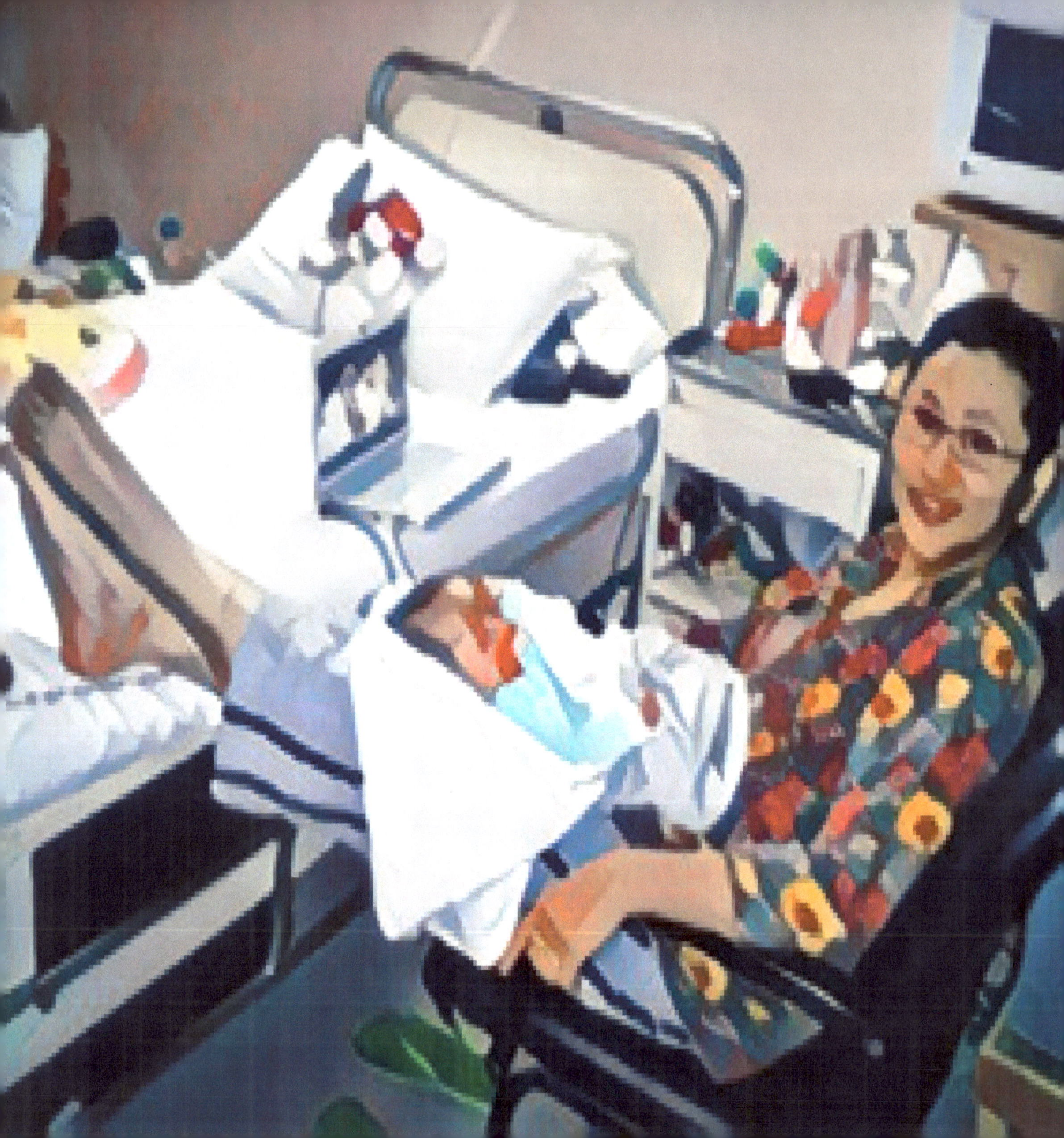

Nine days in the hospital
With mummy by his side,
He decided to recover quickly
Since his mummy often cried.

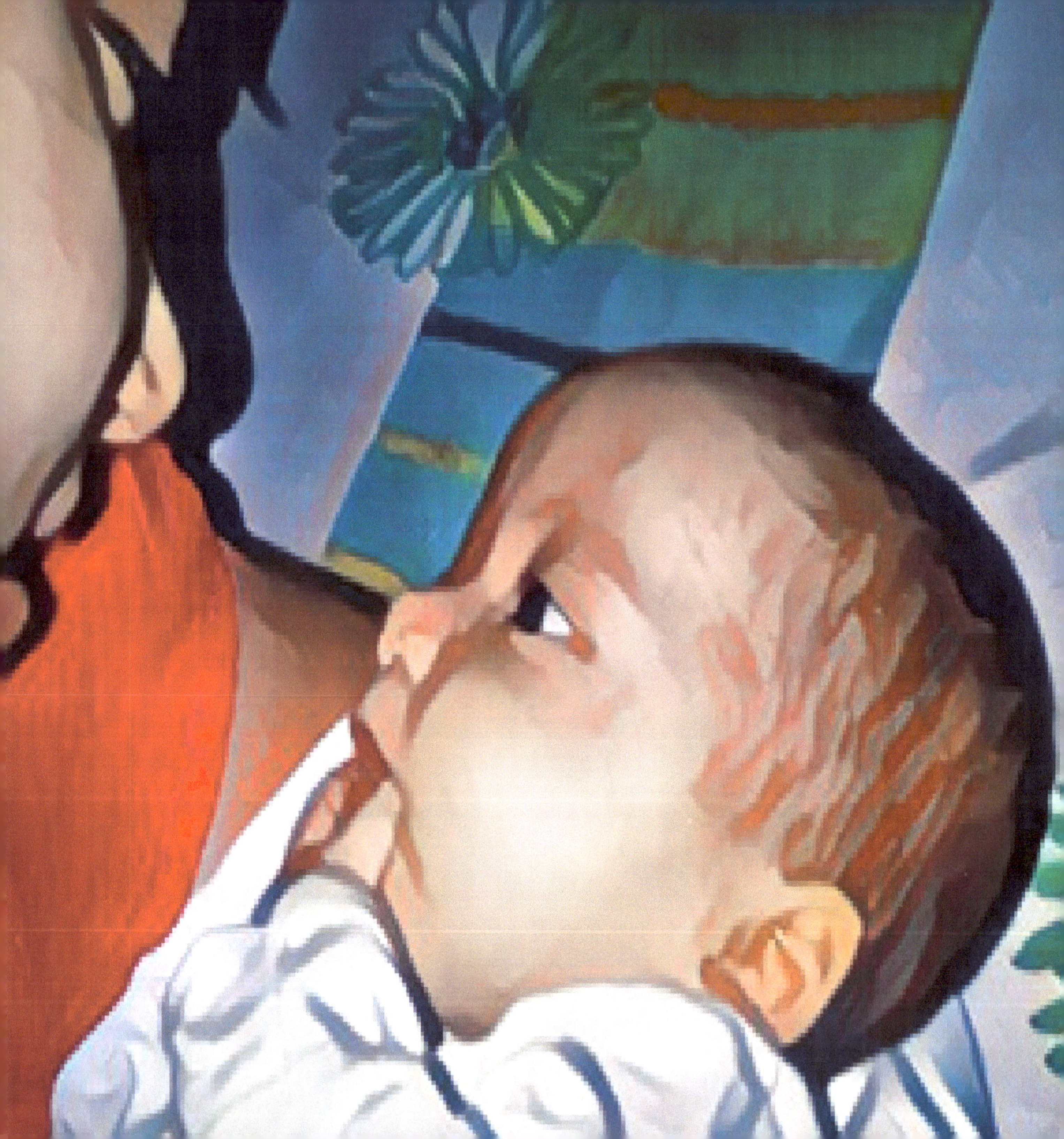

Soon enough, both the little boy and his mummy went home.
They shopped and ate and were free to roam.
Memories were made and photos were taken
Little did his mummy know,
That her whole world would be shaken.

Although brave and strong,
The little boy was getting weaker.
But that did not stop him
From being a loudspeaker!

The little boy would sing and shout
Sounding all the trumpets up in the clouds,
Calling for his mummy out loud,
"PLEASE, CARRY ME AROUND!"

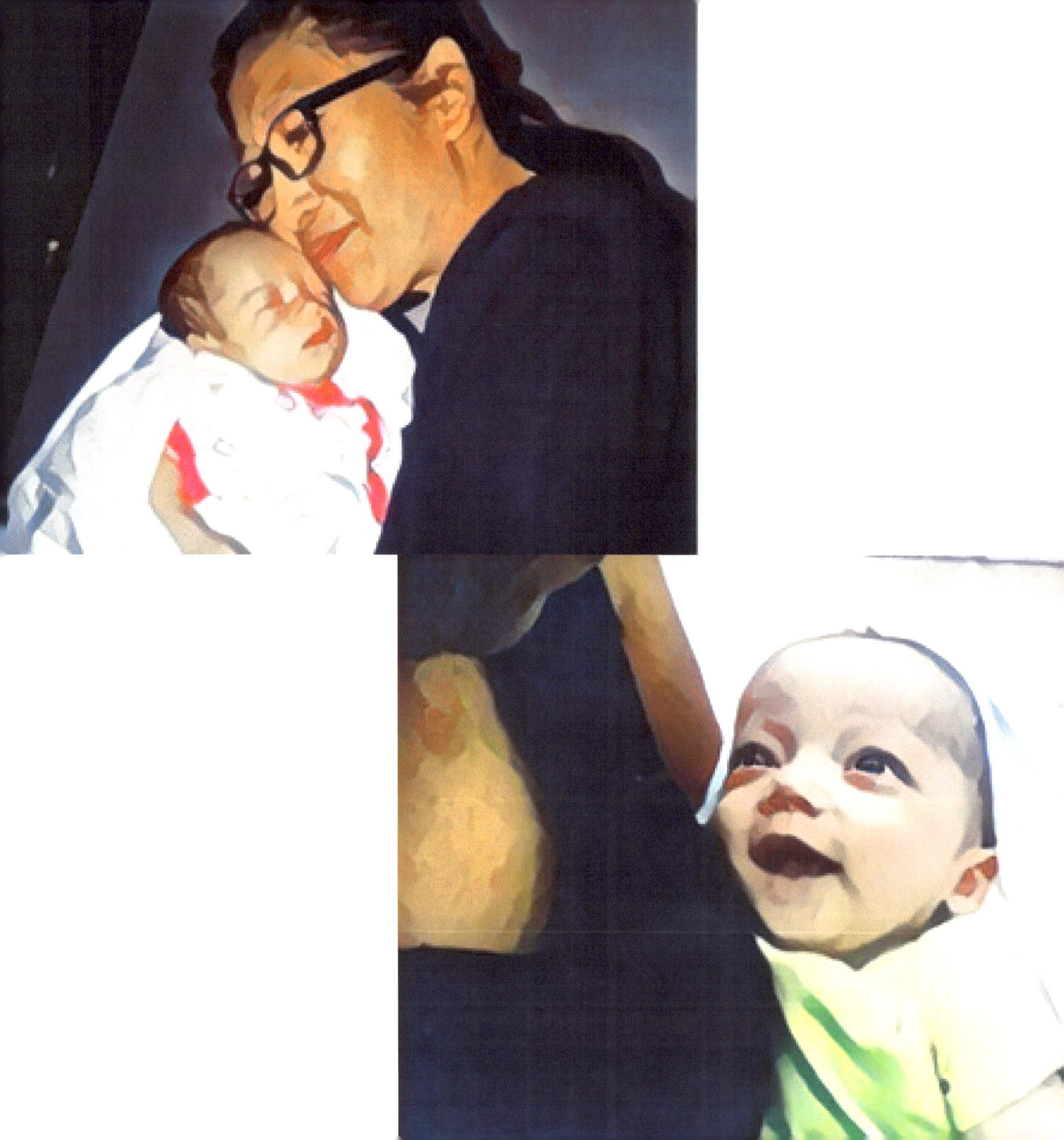

He loved a cuddle with his Api,
Her warm embrace and soothing words,
Always made the little boy happy.

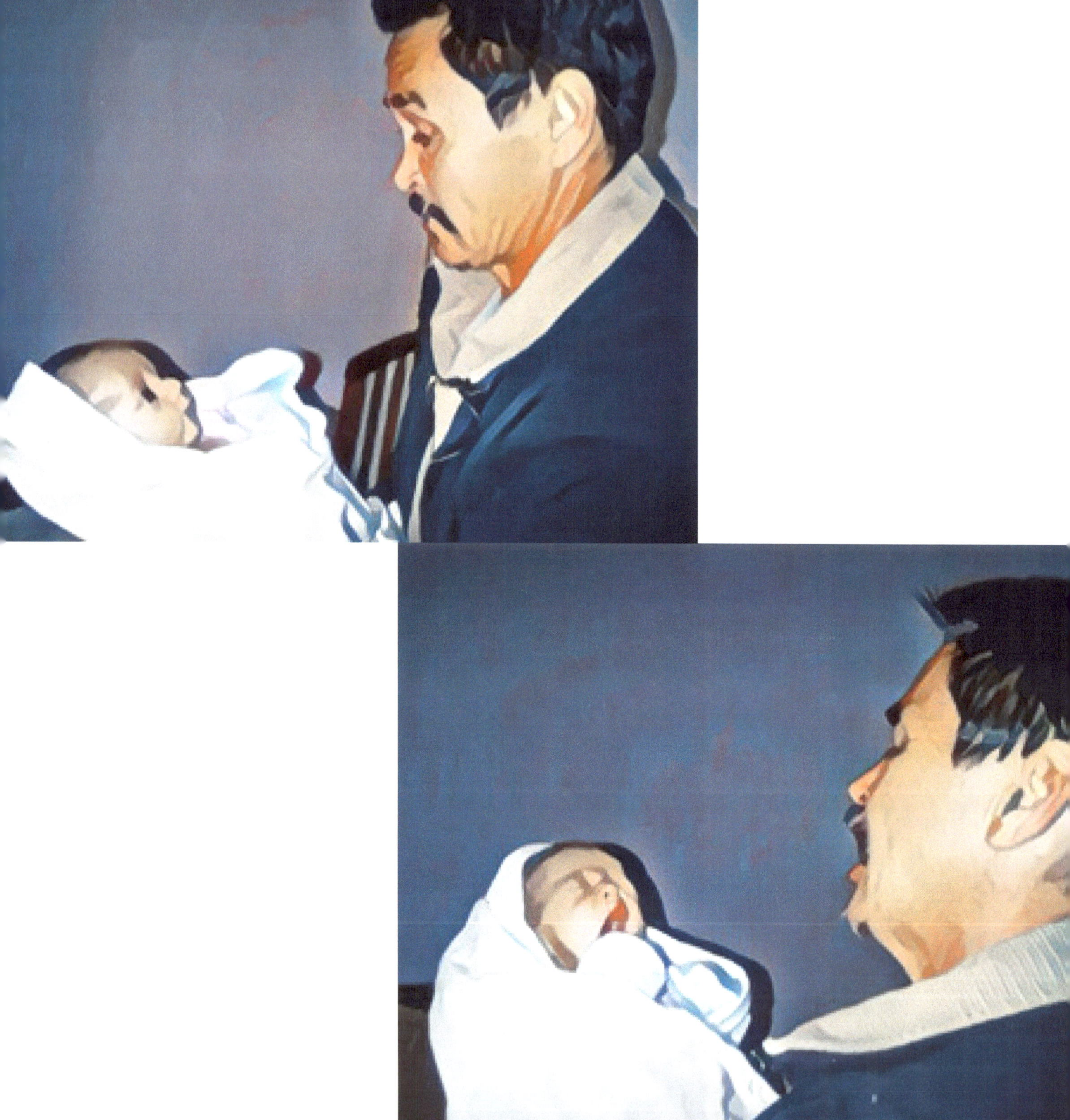

And Grandpa was his best friend,
Always by his side.
He promised the little boy he would always provide.

And Grandpa kept his promise,
Even after the end.

As days went by
Until the last day of July,
The little boy was much loved.
Especially for six months and three days,
He was mummy's beloved.

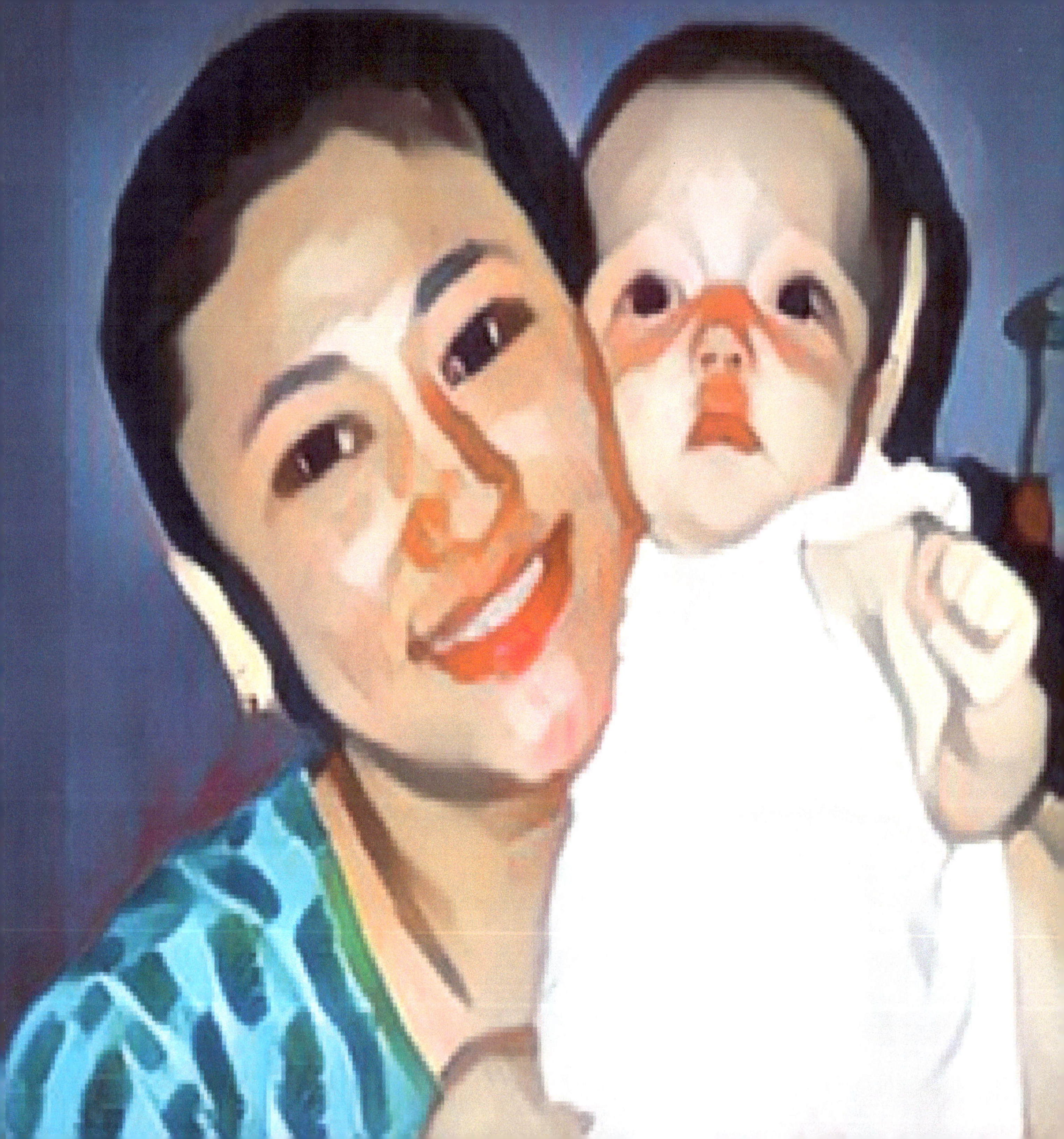

His mummy stood at heaven's door to protest,
"This is not funny!"
Only to be met with,
"It's ok", "Time will heal", by many.

In forty-eight hours
His mummy's world collapsed.
While the little boy in heaven,
Happily danced.

For six months and three days
The little boy did bless.
“Thank you for choosing me”,
His mummy would later confess.

Months and years have passed
Since the little boy fell asleep.
"Until we meet again,
Until we all go to sleep."

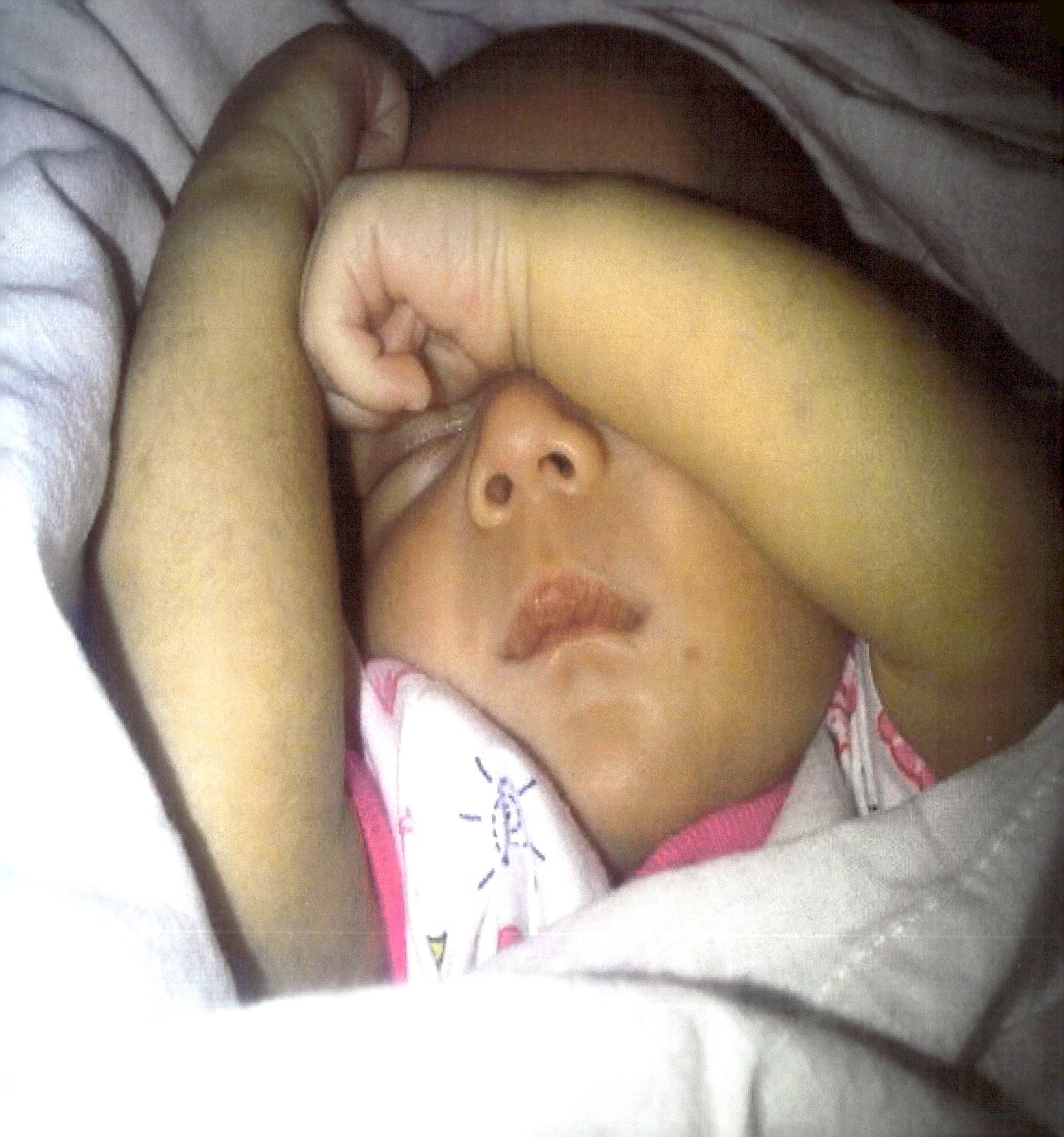

Sweet dreams, darling.

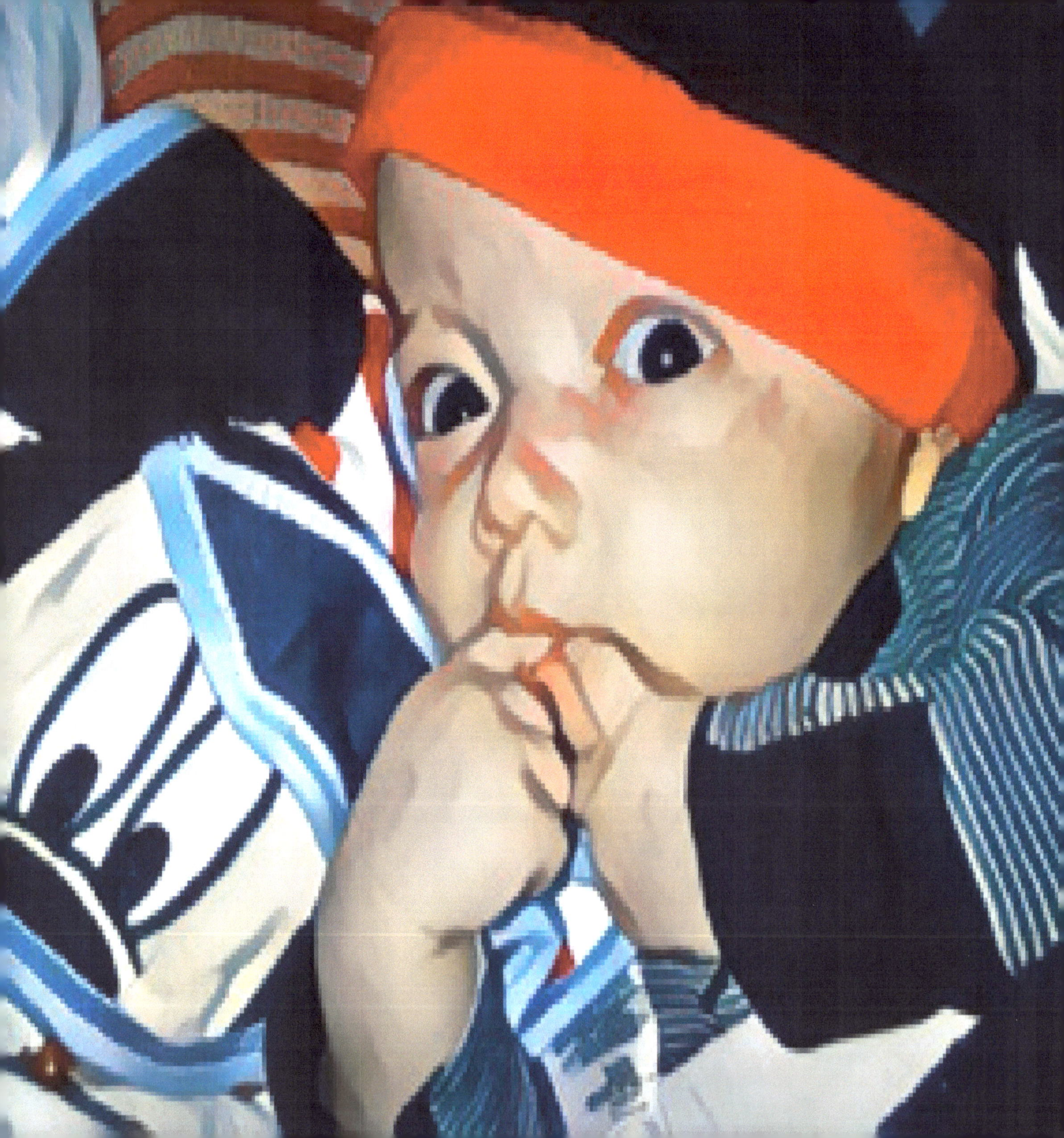

About the Little Boy

Jaisal Michael was born on 28 January 2011 on a sunny Friday morning in Imphal, Manipur in India.

Jaisal weighed 2.9 kilos (6lbs 39oz) and was in the NICU (Neonatal Intensive Care Unit) for seven days until he was ready to go home.

Three days later, he was rushed back to the hospital with seizures lasting more than ten seconds.

He received calcium injections but needed further tests to diagnose him.

He was taken to one of the best and renowned hospital in New Delhi for further tests, diagnosis and treatment.

It took the paediatric specialist .four days, seven vials of blood, multiple scans and X-rays to finally be able to provide a diagnosis for Jaisal.

He was diagnosed with one of the rarest congenital disorder – Malignant Infantile Osteopetrosis (MIOP).

According to Wikipedia, "Malignant infantile osteopetrosis is a rare osteosclerosing type of skeletal dysplasia that typically presents in infancy and is characterized by a unique radiographic appearance of generalized hyperostosis (excessive growth of bone).

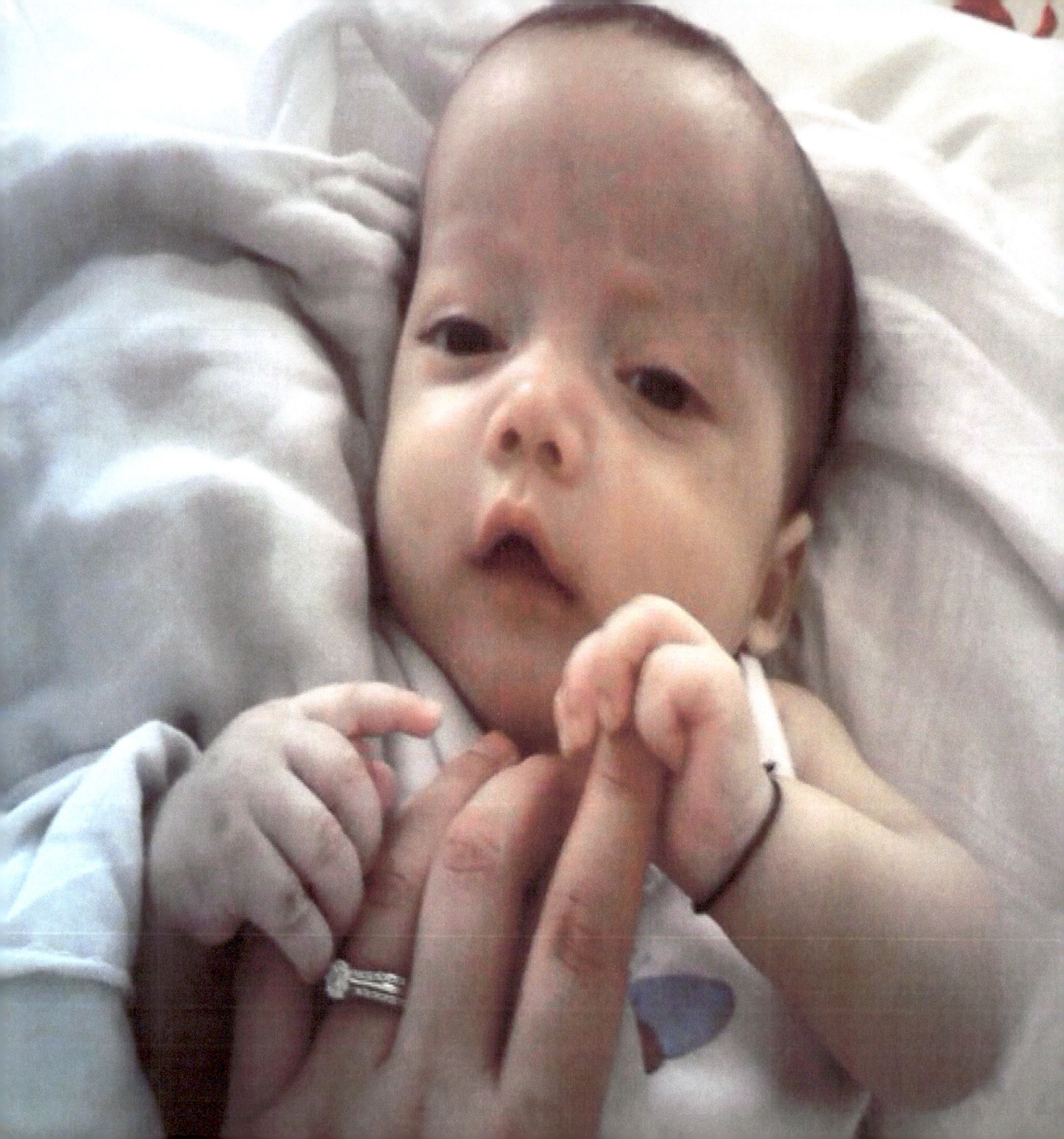

The generalized increase in bone density has a special predilection to involve the medullary portion with relative sparing of the cortices.

Obliteration of bone marrow spaces and subsequent depression of the cellular function can result in serious hematologic complications.

Optic atrophy and cranial nerve damage secondary to bony expansion can result in marked morbidity.

The prognosis is extremely poor in untreated cases. Plain radiography provides the key information to the diagnosis.

Clinical and radiologic correlations are also fundamental to the diagnostic process, with additional gene testing being confirmatory.

Hematologic manifestations related to bone marrow suppression and subsequent pancytopenia are a major source of morbidity and mortality.

Additionally, extramedullary haematopoiesis can result in liver and spleen dysfunction.

Cranial nerve dysfunction and neurologic complications are usually associated with infantile osteopetrosis.

Expansion of the skull bone leads to macrocephaly and, linear growth retardation that is not apparent at birth, delayed motor milestones and poor dentition can ccur."

Jaisal was successful in finding a donor for a bone marrow transplant and before finalising the dates, he fell very ill for two days and two nights.

It was risky for him to travel to New Delhi and in the meantime, his mummy sought help from doctors in Imphal to contain his high temperature.

Unfortunately, Jaisal passed away on 31 July 2011 in his mummy's arms while on the way to the hospital.

He was six months and three days old.

He is still loved and missed by many. He is still his 'Mummy's Beloved'.

About His Mummy

Tammy is Jaisal's mummy.

After 12 years, she is now mummy to three-year-old Ezra and wife to David. They all live in Manchester, United Kingdom.

Tammy is a full-time mummy, a small business owner, an English Language Trainer and, completing a PhD in Linguistics.

She loves to keep busy and if she isn't doing any of the above, you will find her curled on the sofa watching documentaries on Netflix with a large mug of coffee.

The little boy's mummy is forever grateful for all the blessings she's been bestowed with, and for the little angel in heaven looking out for her every day.

The End

www.ingramcontent.com/pod-product-compliance
Lightning Source LLC
LaVergne TN
LVHW071125160826
845679LV00005B/1185
9798890267870